EMERGENCY!

BY GAIL GIBBONS

HOLIDAY HOUSE
NEW YORK

For my friends Randy and Sharon Miller at the
Corinth-Topsham Emergency Response Team of Vermont

Library of Congress Cataloging-in-Publication Data
Gibbons, Gail.
Emergency! / by Gail Gibbons. — 1st ed.
p.   cm.
ISBN 0-8234-1128-1
1. Emergency vehicles—Juvenile literature.   [1. Emergency
vehicles.   2. Vehicles.]   I. Title.
TL235.8.G53   1994   94-2109   CIP   AC
363.3'48—dc20

Emergency! Sometimes people need help.

The people who rush to the scene are specially trained to handle different kinds of emergencies. They want to get to an emergency as soon as possible.

These people use different types of transportation to get there and to assist them in helping to save lives and protect property.

POLICE
MOTORCYCLE

Emergency! Police officers use motorcycles and police cars to speed through busy traffic to go where they are needed. They turn their sirens on and flash their lights to warn other drivers on the road to get out of the way.

POLICE CAR

The police rush to the scene of a crime or accident. Often, calls come from the main office over a two-way radio. Police cars and motorcycles are built to go fast.

Some police use rescue unit vehicles, too. They rush to more complex emergencies.

These rescue units carry equipment, tools and specially trained police officers.

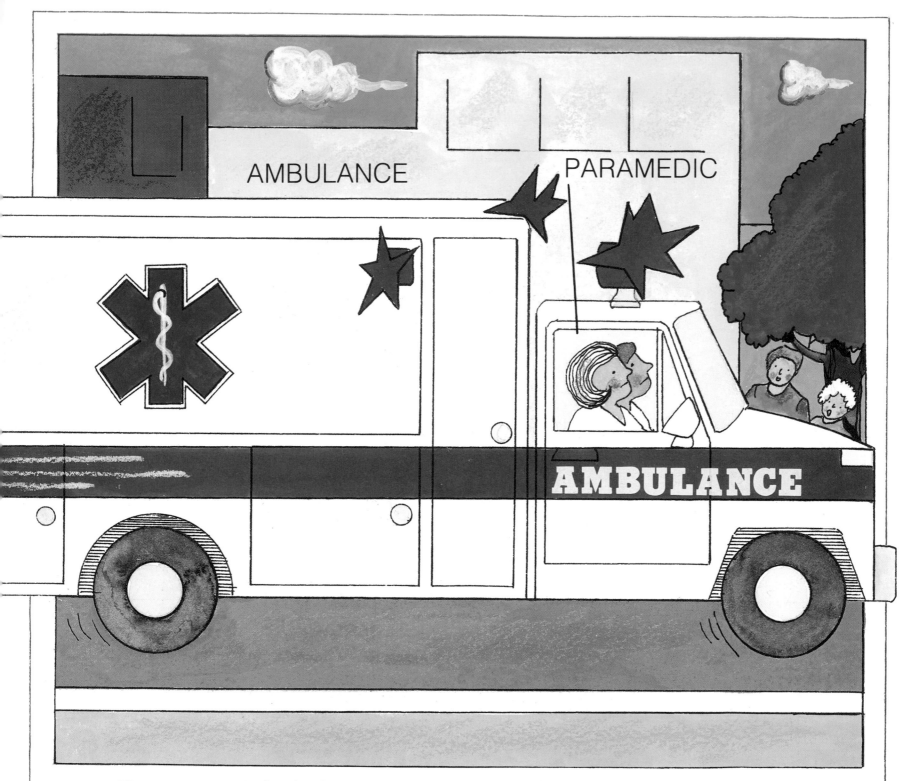

Emergency! Ambulances rush to people who are very sick or injured. The ambulances are staffed with highly trained people called paramedics who give medical help.

Ambulances are equipped with medical equipment to care for and transport patients to hospitals or medical centers as quickly as possible.

Emergency! During terrible storms, power lines may be knocked down. Special utility trucks hurry to the scene.

BOOM

These vehicles carry special equipment and tools to repair the lines. They have booms that lift the workers up in the air.

Emergency! Fire trucks rush to a fire. Different types of fire trucks are used to fight different kinds of fires.

Tanker trucks can fight fires as soon as they arrive at the scene. They carry their own water supply. The fire fighters pump the water through hoses onto the fire.

NOZZLE

PUMPER TRUCK

FIRE HYDRANT

FIRE HOSE

DISCHARGE HOSE

Pumper trucks don't carry their own water. Instead, they pump water from a fire hydrant or other water sources such as ponds, lakes or rivers. The water goes into the trucks through hoses.

The pumps in the fire trucks push the water back out of the trucks and up through the discharge hoses. Streams of water hit the flames.

Fire fighters use two kinds of trucks to reach high places. The aerial ladder truck has an extension ladder with a platform on top. The elevating platform truck uses a boom with a platform.

ELEVATING
PLATFORM
TRUCK

Pipes carry water to the tops of the ladder and boom. Also, both these fire trucks can carry fire fighters up high to save people from burning buildings.

Emergency! Boats are used in emergencies, too. Fireboats are used to fight fires on the water and along the shore. These boats have big pumps that suck in huge amounts of water and force it onto fires.

COAST GUARD BOAT

The Coast Guard uses their boats to rescue people and boats in distress.

POLICE BOAT

POLICE BOAT

Police also use boats when there is a crime or accident.

TUGBOAT

Often, tugboats are used in emergencies. They have equipment on board to help people and ships in trouble.

Emergency! Fire fighters use helicopters and planes to fight forest fires. They drop water and sometimes chemicals to smother flames.

COAST GUARD HELICOPTER

COAST GUARD PLANE

The Coast Guard uses helicopters and planes to rescue people and boats that are in trouble. They are used to fight crime, too.

Often, the police use helicopters to assist in rescues and to fight crime. Many times they can arrive faster at the scene this way.

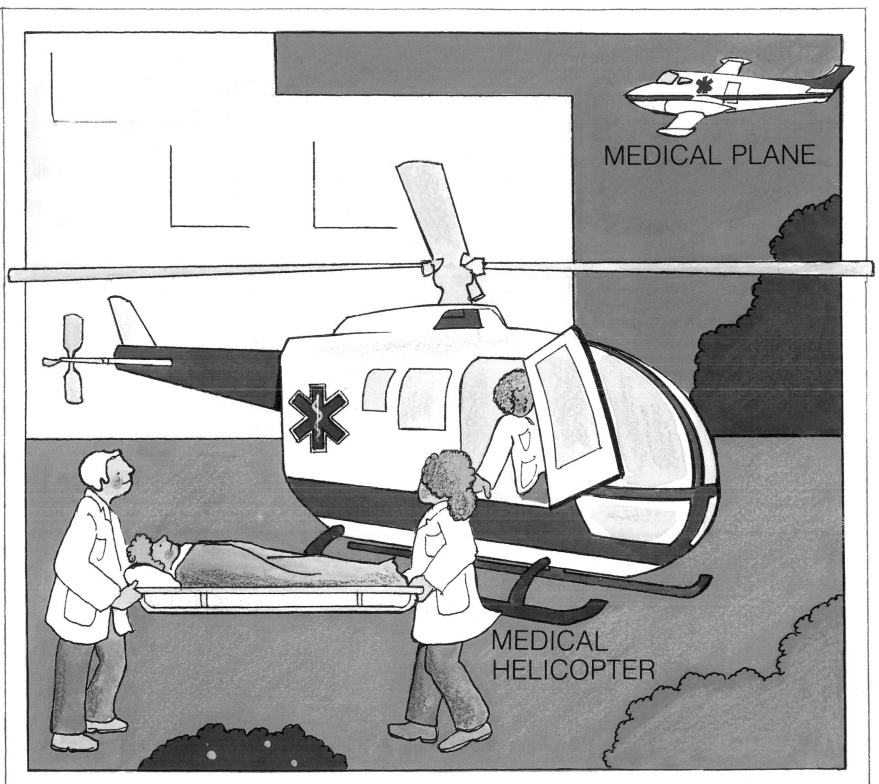

MEDICAL PLANE

MEDICAL
HELICOPTER

Helicopters and planes are used to rush people to hospitals and medical centers, too. They have specially trained people and medical supplies on board just like an ambulance does.

Today emergency workers are able to respond faster and with better equipment than ever before.

Emergency! When there is an emergency, many types of equipment and people leap into action!

WHAT POLICE USED IN THE PAST

—Police used horses to hurry to where they were needed. In some places police still use them.

—The first police vehicles were pulled by horses.

—Police used bicycles, too. They still use them in some places today.

—Later, they used automobiles. This one is a 1935 Chrysler.

AMBULANCES OF THE PAST

—The first ambulances were used to carry wounded soldiers from battlefields. In 1790, two French army surgeons developed what they called the "flying ambulance." It was a converted cart pulled by horses.

—The first peacetime ambulances were used in the 1880s.

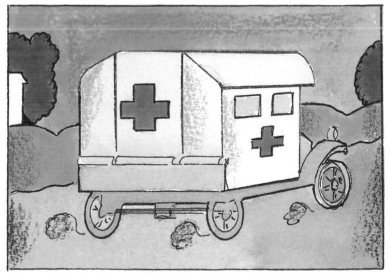

—In 1908, the best ambulances were based on the Ford Model T car.

FIRE FIGHTING VEHICLES IN THE PAST

—In 1721, the first successful fire engine was invented. It had two hand-operated pumps placed in a water tank on wheels.

—At first fire fighting vehicles were pulled by people or teams of horses.

—The first steam engine fire fighting vehicle was built in 1829. This one is from the 1860s. It took time for the water pressure to build up. A fire hose reel and ladders were carried on·separate wagons.

—In the 1890s the first fire fighting vehicles with gasoline engines were used. Horses weren't needed anymore. The engines pumped water immediately.